Light and Shade

Gerry Brennan and Mariana Santos

Light and Shade

ISBN-13: 978-0692508244
ISBN-10: 0692508244

for more books, visit Pski's Porch:
www.pskisporch.com

Printed in U.S.A.

To Walter Sisulu,
who mastered both the light and the shade

Table of Contents

Table of Contents, cont'd

These poems are intended to cover all bases with regards to gender, race, and alienation and ultimately to be inclusive in some small way towards the whole human race.

The poems are rarely about me and my daily grind attempting to be human amidst the chaos of life, not because I'm afraid or reluctant to reveal my inner 'pain', but rather that the macro interests me more than the micro and my own neuroses are of little account as I'm aware that all people, at some level, comprehend all the issues that affect us, so generally my work is bereft of self indulgence as I believe we all suffer things like melancholy, abandonment, and the need to be accepted, and loved.

--Gerry Brennan

All the drawings in this book are drawings inspired by the poems, as opposed to visual representations of them. They're meant to be something that was born out of a poem but that could live by itself.

In these drawings I tried the capture an idea in the poem, the sense of the poem or even an image that was suggested by a particular line.

In some of the poems an image or a number of images would appear instantly and seemed to just fit. In other poems I would come up with less obvious links between poem and image or just have personal take on it.

--Mariana Santos

Slight Refrain

The star spangled banner fluttered high,
in tandem with the Woodstock sway.
And those hands, the ones Dürer would proudly have shook
mutated to a place which we name perfection.
So, the master's hands momentarily became star strangled
at once disassembling then reassembling its metric
in a way that Lincoln himself may well have appreciated.
One nation, one people and one flag.
Seismic shift caused by slight refrain.

Tupelo Honey

Throne ascension to becoming king,
King of a genre awash with errant knights
and regal princes, was indeed a crowning glory.
But a kitsch castle in the middle of Memphis
can be a very lonely place and remove a man
from the very subjects who first bestowed title.
Wrought iron gates and densely constructed walls
both keep without within and within without.
Hamlet never wore blue suede shoes, yet you and he
were both haunted - whether real or imaginary, ghosts do exist.
Those sequined suits at Vegas weren't valiant, Parker as Richlieu,
and so many courtiers and courtesans of dubious motive.
Yet despite the badly fitting, slipping, crown and the imperfect reign
you somehow managed to retain that aura which we label majesty.
The king is dead, long lives the king.

A life abridged, after Ambrose Bierce

From the fourth floor it's really such a long way down,
long enough to see each naked star disabled
by its own remote tenderness, or to almost touch
the unlocked gates of Hades as they swing unhinged.
Too far removed to regale Gods unknown
with endless tales of weep and wind.
From this place there is no sense of dormant wonder
waiting to weave domain, nor concealed portals
to unseen fairy worlds where tales of happiness are spun
in tandem with the need of each distressed heroine,
for in this place, love, or love's dedicated whisper is muted
by detachment and enigma and the residue
of all human debris since her world began.
In this moment, in this place nothing else can be said to exist,
for temporarily, all life has been suspended.
Guardian angels are absent as if vertigo were a blunt sword
in the hands of celestial beings, who, paradoxically,
refuse to negotiate with the living about death.
This instant teeters on the brink of its own inability to subdivide
the juncture into countless unspoilt atoms, each one capable
of rebuilding the world anew with untarnished virgin block,
each one shorn from the empty husk of what might have been.
From the fourth floor, it's such a very long way down.

Coma

In dreams
Achilles lay stone still
as she doused
his near perfect body
with unbroken kisses
yet always bypassing
that same one place.
Awake
he would imagine
searching lips
intruding, probing
that untouchable place
releasing the soothing
of forgiveness,
the dissipation of shame
as tongue and lip
in union, unblemished.

Source

Jack the ripper's mother may have been blameless,
this option must be considered in any analysis.
Gave him endless and unbridled love
and sense too of right and wrong.
Told him that all women were God's creatures
and how each of us in turn had flaws.
By the same token, Jack's father too may have loved the boy,
held his tiny hand for dear life as they walked
the back streets of Whitechapel on grey, rainy nights
when unwashed women took silver from unwashed men
with apparent gratitude.
Jack, even at this early stage may have been his own man,
sought order in social chaos,
wondered if the glint of steel might not wreak calm
and purpose in the endless fog.
This is all of course supposition
as he may have been an orphan too.

Ghosts

Ghosts
explain their presence
by reference
to a past
that is proven,
nailed in time.
A fixed point
immutable
for eternity.
Never to be
products
of evolution.

Madeleine

Building sandcastles
can be treacherous
when broken waves and
shattered souls congregate.
Footsteps that give off no sound
leave no trace, no remnant.
Some things have no meaning,
no answer and no promise.
Such actions are beyond the point
where reason and purpose collide.
Destruction and fragility co-exist
but that is not to understand
why hope is named a flightless bird
and left no forwarding address.

Tagestour

Words like throng and cram and suffocate
of themselves explain little, if anything at all.
So we must add to it thread by broken thread,
layer by invisible layer
using words as though we had not yet
invented them.
Words like metal and train, bake and burn
menstruating woman in hot August sun.
And the words which we omit are as valid
as the words which we choose.
So we shall not give vision to cool soft winds
or pitchers tall with crushed ice water
nor give sound to crisply laundered linen
or suggest vase for freshly cut rose.
Behind every single half impression
that we may have managed to vaguely evoke
lie images too enmeshed in the weave
to ever begin carry things other
than the fragile ghost of the message.

In ash

In ash
we reduce
what was not
into
what could never be.

In ash
lies memory
and energy
converted to nothing,
more or less.

In ash
lies admission
of mortality
and finite.

In ash
no music
or sound.
No decibel
to wake
what almost was.

In ash
sits the problem
to all our answers.

Biko

I see you
a long time ago
stalking
dusty roads
somewhere
in old England
face covered
by mask of silk
glad given
by some lady
whose nights you stole
and her diamonds too.
But she forgave you,
somehow sensing
in that vague way,
or the look in the eyes
she could not see
that you could die
for a cause
that your outlaw soul
found richer
than all the diamonds
yet to be stolen.

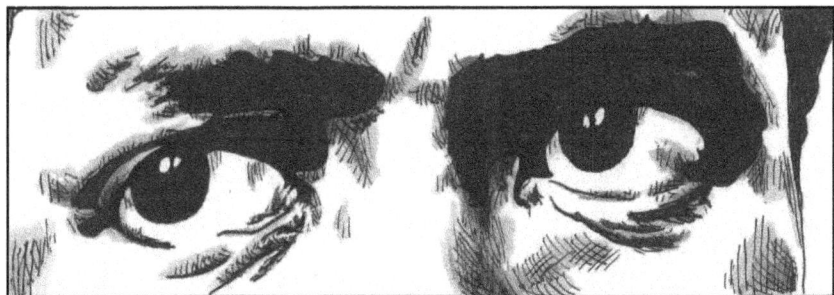

Because the world is round

We
in the flat earth society
hold vigils
for those
who use geometry
to garner reason
from a void
that has no circumference

Abortion No.2

The girl alone
walks steady
the street of curves,
for footprints
have no past.
Times dead
betray
times living.
The girl alone
looks to the stars
big and twinkling
and begs them
understand
but the stars
conscious of their breadth
and bright
are beyond reach
of things but born,
so they give no clue
as the girl alone
skirts the margin
of her blood milky
way.

Wax

I learned to kiss your lips
a thousand years before
in some consecrated dream
that endlessly played sounds
I thought I could hear.

I learned to kiss your mouth
in some future time
pinpointed by light years
and all the darkness
they dare suggest.

I learned to unlearn
the sway of mouth and lip
in what we call the now,
the bite, the bit, the how,
the things that come around.

Blind date

In the endless dark
I seek your eyes
to gaze upon me
or simply acknowledge
that I once existed
outside of the cameo
printed in your memory.

Cicero and Luther King

Cicero and Luther King
talked too much
or so it seemed
to some assassin,
standing coy
soft protected by
some loose velvet drape.
In endless split moments
as the shadow of chaos hovered,
each assassin's mind
may have wondered about posterity
as it methodically meandered
through childhood days
when wooden toys
still carried the fragile thread
of possibility and chain.
Oratory however sweetly parsed
is matchless
for dagger drawn
or bullet bridged.
The history of now
is written by action
whilst the history of later
is written by word.
Cicero and Luther King

conveyed sound beyond word
and word conveyed by sound.
All the best assassins
leave but the footprint of sound,
or a simple drape
blowing apologetically,
with the action and sound
of words yet to reverberate.

Proxy war

Would you send
your son to die
helping defend
some square mile
of lush green land
belonging to a noble people.
Would you send
your son to die
for an acre of scrubland
farmed by a man
whose tongue
has no taste.
Would you send
your son to die
for a square metre
of grey dry dirt
that stray dogs
refuse to mark
as territory.
Or would you prefer
to send some other's son
to die for places
whose names
you cannot pronounce
unassisted.

Flags as yet unfurled
remain just cloth
yet to be embroidered
with the unspilt blood
of all the sons.

Lisboa

We watched her city,
not in a dream
but in concrete and gold.
The architecture proud
and lean and full of
aesthetic wonder
mingled with the decay
of ghostly conquistadores
always riding onward,
slaughter at the ready.
Blueprint for the grandeur
of destruction.

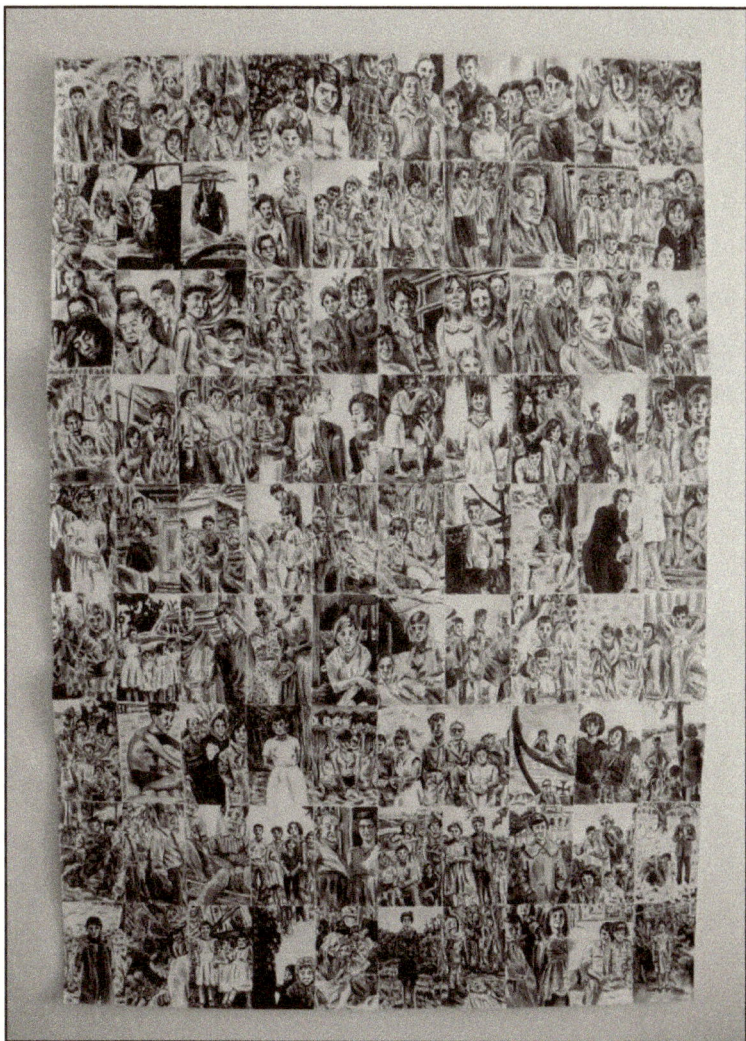

Fractal

I see the butterfly
devoid
of smash and grab,
and I wonder
if it has motive
but lacks means.

Speer

He made a dolls house
for the guards daughter
at Spandau.
She marvelled
at the nooks and crannies
and the way each little thing
just seemed to fit.
Even the lampshades
seemed almost real.
But her tiny face dropped
when she looked but to see
an empty cradle, unrocked.

At Sherwood

In the market place, maid Marian shopped frugally.
Her husband had told her ' we must set an example '.
Each of her children in turn wore hand-me-downs
that had originated as cast-offs,
which Robin's largesse had purchased in the first place
for some downtrodden yokel, a victim of the times.
Yet her man worked hard, of that there was no doubt,
some day's the haul was truly spellbinding in it's array,
large leather purses overflowing with gold coin of the realm
and carved goblets of finest silver, bejewelled to boot.
The hours he spent divining, just to whom
such regained things belonged.
He admitted the problem contained abstraction
and that there was no perfect solution.
Only the man who toils with the sweat of his brow
delivers product worthy of recompense
therefore all gold must truly be his.
She had countered to the effect that a mother who raised
and washed and cooked must surely equate
but he seemed oblivious to this point.
Whenever the Sherwood wives got together to grumble
she found herself apologising for that awful green attire
he made their men folk wear and her use of the word camouflage
simply fell upon the deafest of ears.
At the Sheriff's ball each year they'd arrive, uninvited

through a backdoor or an unguarded cellar
so she'd never get the chance to show off
the little black number that she'd run up herself
from the wasted gown of some dead friar Robin knew.
When the merchants too were doing well
their wives would walk by her, slyly whisper 'communist'.
The peasants to whom he would only refer to as noble
adored him and more, think veneration and awe
for these were the things that they brought to his altar.
At night Robin lay by her side exhausted by exertion
of bringing justice to a world without enlightenment
or returned from some perilous trek to save the neck
of someone or other from the gallows or the rack.
Long gone the days when his sinewy frame served only
to exhaust itself in the service of liberating her from coy virgin ways.
So in her makeshift settlement built of straw and twig
from the damp forest floor she could but dream of Persian rugs
upon which her regal feet would never tread
or of magic lamp beyond the touch of her once graceful fingers.
More than once she played the game of wondering
what kizmet may have spun at the hands of Nottingham
with his primal urge to possess her at all cost
and if possession and love could ever be connected
in a man devoid of vision and vision's reason.
He had sneered as he told her of those strange, deluded souls

who in obsession seek justice and castle for each and every man.
They need this thing for they cannot accept the poetry of chance
nor can they live la dolce vita.
Nottingham, to her immense surprise read verse, especially
the Rubaiyat of Omar Khayyam.
I as sheriff would sew diamonds to your skin
for gold alone would be unworthy of proximity to you..
And she wondered if such shallow words hid deeper meaning
as if an enigma she must unwrap.
I will not build you castles in the air nor will I sacrifice a single strand
from your fair hair to save a multitude whose eyes don't shine my way.
Poetry was, according to Robin, an abandonment
an admission that words were more important than action.
A sword, he had told her would change history far quicker
than elegies of words parsed to fit in places they did not belong.
Hard stripped, laid bare, this then had been the choices
a dreamer in whose dream's she was essential
but simply as supporting character
or a crazy lord who sought to deify her as the ultimate prize
at some Romanesque orgy transferred to the English midlands.
Truly this is the darkest of dark ages.

Once I saw

Once I saw
an art historian
put a Reuben's
under a microscope.
With a scalpel of hindsight
dissecting her breast
in the twentieth century
concluded
that she had been
in the early stages
of breast cancer.
Her face showed no knowing
as the master's brush strokes
immortalised her
in that way
a mammogram could never do.

In Utero

Everyone's mother should surely have felt
the sweet sensual lash of soft black silk
at least one time in a life heavy of toil.
Symbolically, Marie Antoinette did so.

Everyone's mother should surely have bathed
with the sinful touch of asses milk
playfully assaulting their weary limbs.
Legend suggests Cleopatra so did.

Everyone's mother should surely have died
in the wide open arms of some Casanova
for even just one single night,
as volunteers seemingly had few regrets.

Everyone's mother once walked virgin
and this includes all those Mary Magdalens.
Everyone's mother had the courage to bleed
as did the teenage Joan at Orleans.

Everyone's mother somehow gave birth successfully
between one and many, all in real time.
In essence everyone's mother remains as ghost
to all the mothers.

Manequin

Sometimes I remember
to forget about you,
and all those broken promises.
The ones, if ever laid end to end
would make the milky way blush.
Other times I forget that memory
bequeaths but illusion and how
what is and what was converge
to a point that has no purpose
beyond the way we choose
to dress it's dot.

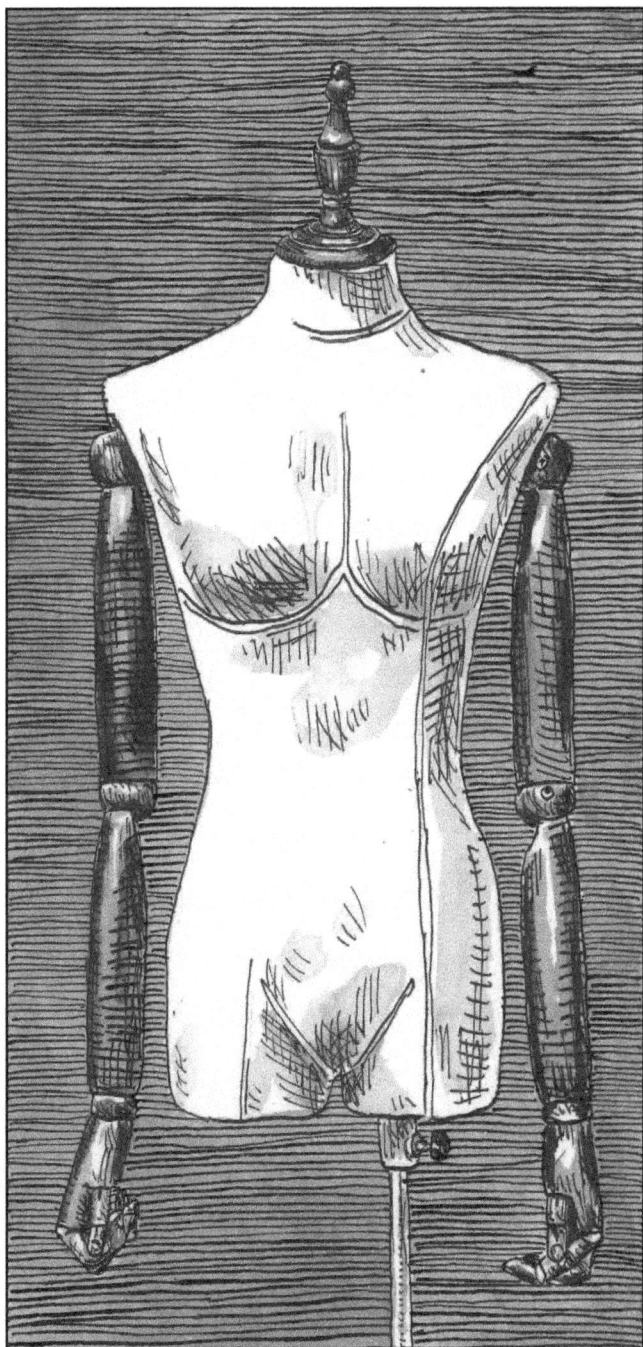

Change

She said that she remembered escudos
how one always had so many
even when absolutely poor.
Said it made them all feel like somebody
to spend a hundred here or a thousand there.
The notes it appears compliment each other
in texture, size and shape.
So to carry them made her feel protected,
almost safe.
Now they have gone the way of antiquity
to take their domain between relic and ruin.
Sometimes progress makes us feel stranded
between the prairies and the wolves.

Chelsea Hotel

I could have been a motel,
and Marlon could've stayed there.
Neolithic horses with their neo-gothic carriages
hauling up all the would be's, could be's.
or even Richard the third
swapping some horse he never quite found
for a pile of red bricks, too many to count.
I was tall once, even the tallest, when Empire States
were nothing but still-born embryos
on some draftsman's board as they wondered
if Victoria would drop suitcase and trunk,
making royal declarations
to share queenly four poster with Lenny and Janice,
provided fellatio stayed off the menu.
I could have entertained inbred blue bloods
whose gown and train did justice to
my legendary staircase whose steps in number
almost matched the suicides and fatal footfalls nearly taken.
Poets, beat poets, born too young to help defend Stalingrad
or dodge the endless Normandy ricochet,
too old to wear bobby socks for ol' blue eyes
as he chose the Astoria's blue curls of smoke,
filled up my portals with delusions that only chaos begets art
or the illusion that decadence is anything other than by-product.
In my rooms lie beds, but I'm cognizant of the fact

that all who lay head here fell short of Shakespeare
(O for a sister hotel Stratford, circa 1600).
Pop culture and Gothic redbrick form an uneasy alliance,
just ask Warhol - and dreams unmade and dreams unfinished
both unravel when stone and stick gain precedence
or serve as deeper testimony than endless laundered sheets
torn from the bed by chambermaids too poor
to buy their three day pass to Woodstock.

Pyramid

Worthless chunks
of senseless stone
painfully chiselled
by knuckles, gnarled
with someone's vision
of aesthetics et. al.
Limbs bare, bloody,
battered,
shuffle shamelessly
into majesty's snare.
Broken backs feed
suffocated screams,
as rituals claw their way
through eternity unheard,
save for tourists
measured shutter speed.

Modem

The Montagues and the Capulets forbade touch
and the internet and things that could depict lust.
Yet the balcony scene lies littered with debris,
hotwired with images of how far virtual bodies stretch.
The Capulets and the Montagues knew love's media
is finite, only when the humming heart beats no more.

A page from the diary of Mrs. Crusoe
(after Carol Duffy)

The night before he sailed
my man Robinson told me
that though he loved me, he needed time, time alone.
The voyage, he said, would give much needed
time to think, to reflect, to do those things
a man must do to clear his head.
Space according to him was but a concept
that we should not be afraid to embrace.
He talked of alienation and how one could use it
as catharsis rather than chore.
Now he's gone from the earth
and all of its faces.
On dark nights when I think of him
laying deep and still for all time
I force myself to dream of some island calm
and a sole survivor by miracle from shipwreck
who now finds home in sand and sun.
And I hope too that it's not too crowded
by squawking natives shattering his tranquil bliss.
Just time and space man's two great enemies,
as much wanted companions
to while away hours that would otherwise drag endless
like some clock made from infinite grains of sand.

To Somehow

To somehow separate
longing from belonging
is a complex thing.
Longing is the crisp fall leaf
we simply have to crunch,
the parched, cracked soil
that begs us water,
a melody that must be hummed.
Belonging is of other things.
Black empty days
and unbroken nights
when cut adrift from blood and bone,
we float by extinct ghost
as words of fragile and feather
remain too heavy or gauche
to even begin articulation
of any splintered ruin.
This is when, if ever,
we feel belonging's mouth
its wet, warm kiss
loose of explanation
and unseeking of prediction
or the promise of a past.

Words of love

All words of love are but nothing
a clever arrangement of sounds
from my lip to your ear
aimed at synchronising
with some piece of you
which I imagine
seeks liberation from
the burden of being unloved.
All words of love are but chains
(sometimes forged of nobility)
carefully laid links
to tie bonder with the bonded.
All words of love carry possibility
that woven into their mix
(beyond the syllables)
are raw, perfect things
accidentally capturing
those things I feel for you.

Rapunzel (for AR)

Rapunzel
take out that scissor
blade, shank or shiv
go blindly hacking,
loosely sacking
for in this moment
there is no aesthetic.
Let each tress meet abandon
and the lyric of mutilation
with its shaft of hysterical calm.
Then tie each looping strand
to a thing that must be heavy
or use as metaphor
the rusting anchor of your soul,
now swing without measure
down
down
down.
Touching soil you must beware
for every space has different perils
flush with errant princes
loitering with the intent
to swap freedom for tiaras
and all those things
that make the world a tower.

Nation

Nation
an artificial
construct
men
die for.
Nation
a line
on a map
drawn
in blood.
Nation
a hem
to keep
within
without.
Nation
a soil
to live off
and bury
too.
Nation
a square
triangle
to circle
one.

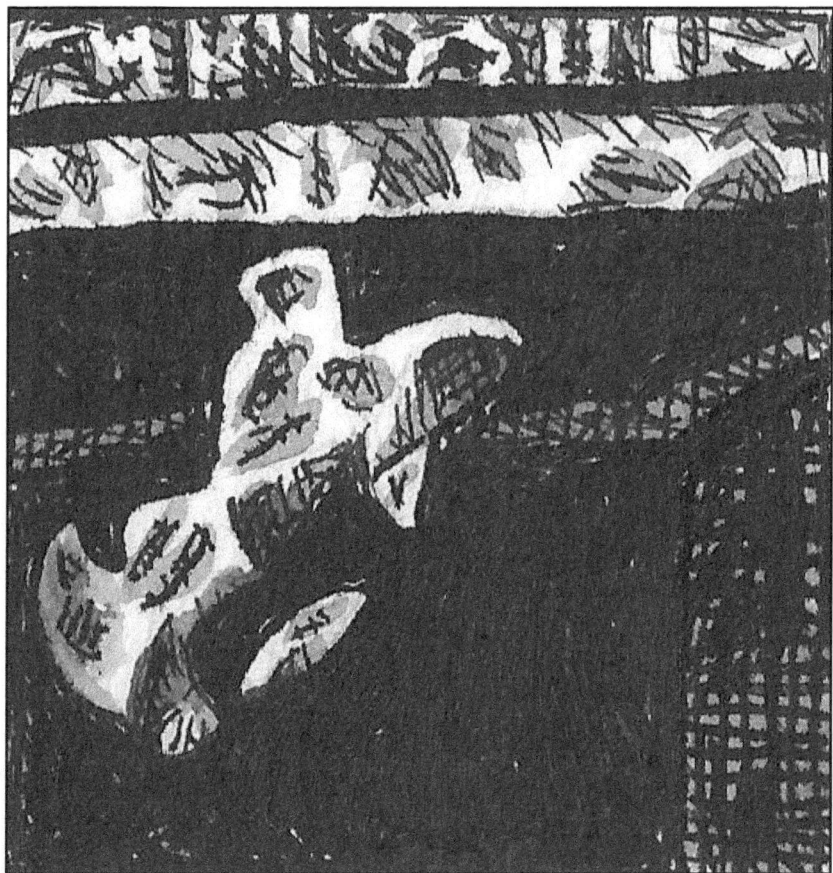

67

Valentine

I could not with certainty recognise your shadow
in a room with just two shadows
much less your silhouette as it frantically scrambled
for the safety of a lifeboat
in a raging sea swell on a pitch black ocean
with an unkind moonlight.
In a gallery stained with cold marble floor
and elegant Doric column
your portrait, even carrying your name,
on a well polished brass plate
would induce some small degree of uncertainty
as to if you were really you
and in a cliche spun legend
where the princess brushed her hair the way you do
and shared identical taste in belt, buckle and brocade, I'd still wonder
whether the essence of you was conveyed beyond doubt to my sense
of what I imagined you ever were in the very first place.
In even the best love stories
only fragments of what were initially fragments,
only seeds of what were once seeds,
and only hints of what may have been suggestions,
remain.
These words then carry the inference
of what could almost be a declaration of love
from me to you.

Eve's story

I can only remember those first days
as a landscape of indelible beauty,
different each time we glanced
as though responsive to our mind's eye.
The broad expansive dawns
with their endless haze of rich dewy mist
that induced involuntary breathlessness
just by their raw fragile sense of wonder.
In clockless timed meander
unburdened by the back of history
and blameless yesterdays
we were truly untroubled, almost free.
We foolishly imagined that winds only blew
in accordance to our mood of whim
and that rains could only ever nourish.
It seems a truism that all is relative
but this is not so, for even then
we sensed that this was indeed paradise.
All fruits were ripe to our bite
and all movement of limb was easy.
There was no wrong way to be
no order
no disorder
simply endless joy unfolding in a continuum.
We rarely used words,
not because we couldn't
but because speech seemed unnecessary.
All was obvious.
There was no concealment.
There was no repression.

There was no shame.
Couples collide in such strange ways
and we were no exception.
I awoke as from an eternal slumber
and there he was
dizzy with expectation,
and at this birth of romance
we both at once knew nothing
as nothing was everything.
Although I had no statue of Adonis
and he no bust of Helen
we at once understood perfection.
Our skins of different colour
seemed to match in a harmony
that belonged to us and to us alone.
And all we did was touch as all touch was wanted.
Inseparable, sublime ecstasy layered upon
ecstasy.
Floating when awake, alert when at sleep.
Essence of bliss being permanent, fixed, immutable.
Time's passage now gives me some perspective
and gives name to sensations I had thought as nameless.
We were naïve and innocent as things of beauty must be.
Thought there was no right way up.
This suspended state of Nirvana retained its own momentum
but for how long I cannot say as we did not know of when.
People always ask about our fall and this I understand.
Schadenfreude is part of what we are
and perhaps what we should seek to tame.
Within every tale there is fact and fable
and each seeks to exonerate their own.
Impulses may destroy us or enhance us
but they are always of the moment

as though meditation kills our right to be of now.
I may surprise by stating that my tale as told
by men with long grey beards is largely accurate
and save for minor details, their writ is true.
However history is not told with the tender sweep
of the artist's brush and the historian's pallet is more
concerned with form than texture,
so to this extent I simply seek to retouch the canvas
of what and why and who I was,
all of course within the limitations of self knowledge.
I have no ideology nor am I religious
but contained within that paradox remains the fact
that I was touched by God and in turn sought to return touch.
Therein lies the seed of my fall.
It was a plant and not an apple of which we partook
but that is not to trivialize a tale which is right in much regard.
And as I have already sung, all was cast to perfection;
until one time twixt night and dawn,
I had awoken as the man slept on.
I watched his body in its exquisite stillness
save for the soft even breaths it expelled
and in that moment I sensed within his naked frame
a vulnerability that stripped me bare,
a place deep inside which I had not known till then.
The feeling filled me up to overflow
and after its initial tremor had subsided
there remained some residue which I could not displace
for it lodged as though now a part of what I was and
what I had become,
this was the first secret known to humankind
but not the last.
Later, Adam too sensed the change
but rather than resist it, he embraced it

and if anything seemed to desire me evermore.
It was he who coined the term woman
as though Eve no longer fit.
So that day in question
the one that scholars overanalyze
was not unlike the ones before.
God did indeed specifically ask of us
not to partake of that particular plant
and as usual we nodded our consent
for we always sensed his power
such immense power
and his tenderness
such immense tenderness
and yes it was a serpent who served as catalyst
and suggested that forbidden things must have their worth
and so to so sup could but enhance us,
enrich us
endow us
enlarge us.
I do not know what went through the head of Adam,
for who can tell with men
but for my part I did indeed sense that by partaking
I would in ways be God's equal, his peer,
enter his domain
share his burden
communicate in holy tongues
touch a sacred thing
within a thing,
who had scattered stardust amongst an infinite cosmos.
In that instant I sensed God's fragility, bareness
an utter sense of being alone through all the ages
and felt awash with joy at thoughts of giving solace
to his untouched soul.

Insane.
Inane.
Profane.
But that is as it was.
I remember too its moonlit night
when all was filled with calm and stray.
Adam was off collecting butterflies
or whatever it is that men do when away from our domain,
and God spoke to me without exchanging words.
Conveying to me that I was perfection,
all of me.
From my wicked sparkling eyes
to my full round breasts.
My strong , steel-like spine and
my mouth as sensuous as though lips carved from nothing-
ness
could but contain everything.
How my back formed a miraculous arch when I was love.
He said I had things which Adam could never possess
and how poetry should always be rewritten.
That nothing in the thing called space
could ever hope to match my wound of being.
I felt enthralled, ensconced, enraptured
tingling without origin or end,
in short, I felt seduced.
He was endlessly unfolding petals
ones which my dear Adam did not know had seed
let alone could ever flourish to a bloom.
My desire, for that is what it was, to embrace his aura
was unbearable, well beyond the bent of word.
Think desire multiplied by an infinity
then keep on adding till digits go blind.
This was my first and last covenant with God

but what exactly it meant to him, I cannot adequately say.
For in the garden some seed was sown
as a serpent begged me dine
in aftermath I was now mine,
I felt immunized, insulated, immortal.
Limbs which had always carried light now dared lighter still.
I felt aroused yet not for my Adam,
whose advances I spurned for the very first time.
I imagined ,in real time ,of embracing God,
mortal to mortal,
immortal to immortal
of straddling his shapeless being
for him to penetrate my entire
in ways I did not remotely understand
beyond their need.
In this fantasy he willingly lay across my breasts
called them perfect orbs ,the font of all sustenance,
ran fingers through my hair and seemed to sing my name,
our lips would crash in synchronicity with falling stars
but he would not, could not penetrate me as desired,
at once becoming garbled and confused
as if racing through countless oblivions
had run his sap to dry and
left imbalance, for that was the word I sensed he used.
Returning to what I found was named reality
God's wrath was warm,
his ire unbound.
There was nowhere else but out.
Adam, broken, bowed just walked a shuffle
but I looked slyly back at God
in that knowing sort of way
and strode with those imaginary stilettos

clicking out the arrogant sound of parity
of a moment
with my imperfect creator.

En Passant

Someone should have told
Marie Antoinette,
that in eighteenth century France
Queens, statistically speaking,
were far more likely
than peasant women
to lose their heads.
Tiaras and crowns and other things
that glitter, are as food and fuel
to bellies denied the luxury of bread,
and carats of any measure cannot
thwart the guillotine's blade.
In the twentieth century Tsarina Alexandra
may have read often but she never read
French history from two centuries prior,
So her Faberge pendants were powerless
when the snowflakes turned to red.

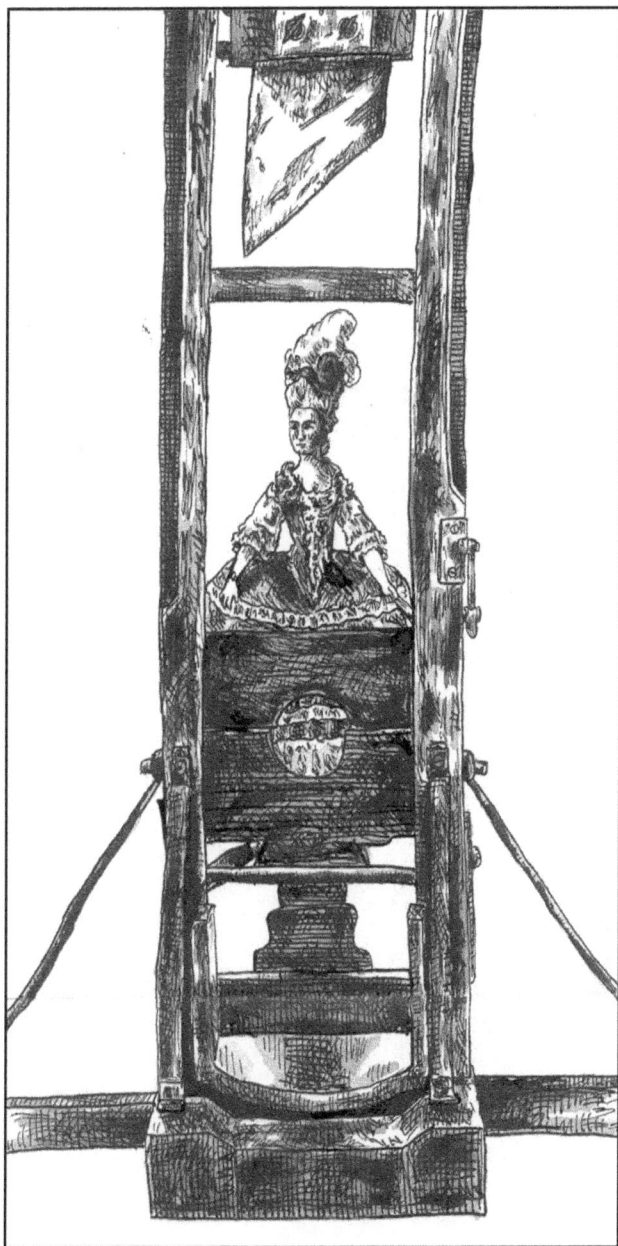

Strange fruit

Each time you sang it, I also lost breath and choked.
I too dying inside and my white face symbolically hanging.
Knowing that each word took a piece of you away with it,
I could not erase your pain but I could share some scintilla.
You paring and baring such visceral words in metaphor
yet each of us knowing that they were of course not metaphoric
and the tenderness of your fragile muse confirming as much.
Such tragedy in beauty but no beauty in such tragedy.
I could almost use a word I loathe, angel.

After reading Wells

In a time machine together
we two shall travel back to far
yet not so far as distant.
A hundred years or so
when horses still had hooves
that beat broken rhythms on stone.
Your role of necessity will be clichéd,
some governess or other
a spinster to the core.
The house which we inhabit
shall be ghost-like gothic
straight from pages of some dime novel.
I shall be a study in vague pensiveness
and you an antidote
with tenderness demure.
There shall be a nursery room
where eerie rocking horse
is swayed by invisible wind
or even unseen hand.
There will be no baby,
no child, no heir
and this is fitting,
for unlived past lives
have no need of future

with its incessant need
to deride and mock crystal balls
that detail things
that have only happened
in undreamt dreams.

You will not at this stage pine
for things like status
or emancipation
for that would be to break the spell
so delicately intricate
that it hangs by threads
too heavy for hands of fairy
to whisper a weave.

Nighttime shall be pregnant
with the lure of predictability
as master and servant
fulfill the role bequeathed to all
who foolishly travel back in time.
This role avers that man nor beast
may step outside the strait jacket
imposed by antique social norms
so you will murmur no decline
for that too would be to thieve
the hands of time's innate right

to be disdainful of future
with its absurd notion
that you should be free to choose
whatever pleasure I dare to lavish
upon your virgin soul.

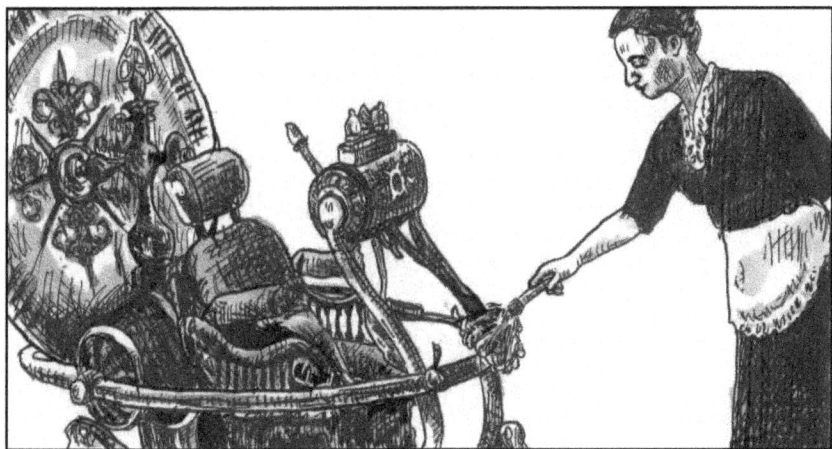

Mariana Santos is from Lisbon and works in figurative art, ceramics and wood engravings. She has had a ceramics piece exhibited in the National Ceramics tile Museum here, and also sculpts and can basically do just about everything artistically with her hands.

Gerry Brennan follows in the cliched tradition of the drunken, Irish poetic tradition and has been in 'exile' for over seven years from his native Dublin. He has just completed a novel, which has an interior monologue and is relatively short but is sharp and decent and very iconoclastic regarding culture, history, and religion.

Pski's Porch
323 East Avenue
Lockport, NY 14094
www.pskisporch.com

Pski's Porch Publishing was formed July 2012, to make books for people who like people who like books. We hope we to have some small successes.
www.pskisporch.com.